KT-465-777

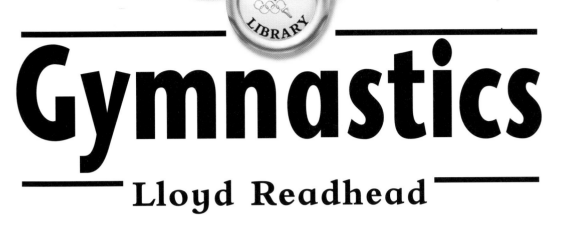

Gymnastics

Lloyd Readhead

Heinemann

First published in Great Britain by Heinemann Publishers
(Oxford) Ltd
Halley Court, Jordan Hill, Oxford OX2 8EJ

MADRID ATHENS PARIS
FLORENCE PRAGUE WARSAW
PORTSMOUTH NH CHICAGO SAO PAULO
SINGAPORE TOKYO MELBOURNE AUCKLAND
IBADAN GABORONE JOHANNESBURG

© Heinemann Publishers (Oxford) Ltd 1996

Designed by VAP Group Ltd
Illustration by Getset (BTS) Ltd (p6).
Printed in the UK by Jarrold Printing, Norwich

00 99 98 97 96
10 9 8 7 6 5 4 3 2 1

ISBN 0 431 05951 9

British Library Cataloguing in Publication Data

Readhead, Lloyd
 Gymnastics. — (Olympic Library)
 I. Title II. Series
 796.44

Acknowledgements
The Publishers would like to thank the following for permission to reproduce photographs:
Eileen Langsley/Supersport Photographs: p.4, 7, 8, 9, 10, 11, 12, 13, 14, 15, 16, 17, 18, 20, 21, 23, 25, 26, 27, 28, 29;
Colorsport: p.5, 24; Agence Vandystadt: p.19; Central Press Photos: p.22.

Cover photographs reproduced with permission of Supersport/Eileen Langsley and Professional Sport
Cover designed by Brigitte Willgoss.

Our thanks to Mr Robert Paul of the US Olympic Committee for his comments in the preparation of this book.

Olympic rings logo reproduced with the permission of the International Olympic Committee.

Every effort has been made to contact copyright holders of any material reproduced in this book.
Any omissions will be rectified in subsequent printings if notice is given to the Publisher.

Contents

Gymnastics at the Olympics

Every young athlete dreams of becoming an Olympic Champion. This book will show what it takes to become a gymnastics star.

Daniela Silivas of Romania, in the 1988 Games, where she won three gold medals.

Developing Gymnastics

In ancient times Romans and Greeks did gymnastics to increase their strength and agility.

Ludwig Jahn in Germany and Peter Ling in Sweden influenced the teaching style of gymnastics around the turn of the eighteenth century. They developed modern gymnastics.

Gymnastic Events

In the early modern Olympic Games, the gymnastic events included high jump and swinging rings. Gymnasts worked on stiff parallel bars and non-sprung floor surfaces. Modern, high-tech apparatus allows gymnasts to demonstrate very complex skills. These exciting performances have made gymnastics into one of the most popular Olympic spectator sports.

Qualifying

The world's top gymnasts qualify for the Olympics by competing at the World Championships in the year before the Olympic Games. The top twelve men's and women's teams qualify to compete in the Olympic Games. Other nations may enter two gymnasts in the **all-around** and individual apparatus events, depending on their ranking at the World Championships.

Vitaly Scherbo, who won six gold medals at the 1992 Games and is therefore the winner of the highest number of gymnastics medals in one Games.

Did you know?

At the Olympic Games, medals are awarded in:

- men's team and women's team championships
- individual all-round titles
- individual apparatus titles.

A male gymnast can win a maximum of eight gold medals, and a female gymnast can win six gold medals. This has never been done. The winner of the highest number of medals in one Olympic Games is Vitaly Scherbo (CIS), who won six gold medals at the 1992 Barcelona Games. Vera Caslavska (Czech), Nadia Comaneci (Romania), Ecaterina Szabo (Romania) and Daniela Silivas (Romania) have each won three gold medals in one Olympic Games.

The first gymnastics clubs started in the United States in 1850, and in England in 1860. Since then there have been many changes to the apparatus used for training and competition. These changes have made gymnastics the spectacular sport it has now become.

A New Beginning

The Olympic Games in Atlanta, USA, mark the beginning of an exciting new period in the development of gymnastics. After 1996, gymnasts do not have to do any compulsory exercises. They can concentrate on the optional exercises. This means that more training time can be spent developing new and interesting skills.

The Competition Arena

At the Olympic Games and other major events the gymnastics apparatus is erected on a raised **podium**. The diagram shows the arena layout for a men's event. In women's events, bars and the beam usually replace the horizontal bar and the parallel bars.

The **judges** sit at floor level around the podium. Electronic score boards are used at the side of the podium to show the judges' scores.

The Apparatus

Gymnasts in the men's artistic competition perform their optional exercises on six different pieces of apparatus. The women competitors perform on four.

Podium layout

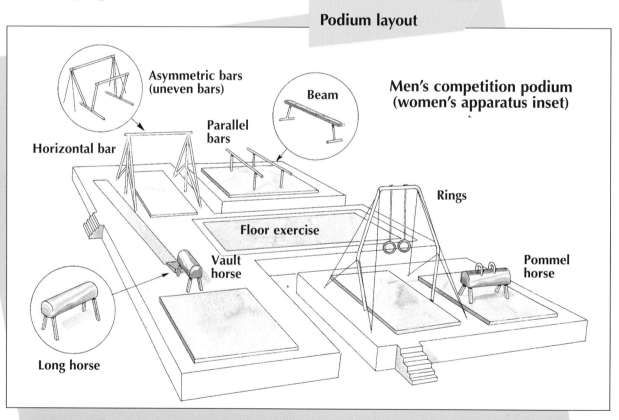

Asymmetric bars (uneven bars)

Beam

Parallel bars

Men's competition podium (women's apparatus inset)

Horizontal bar

Rings

Floor exercise

Vault horse

Pommel horse

Long horse

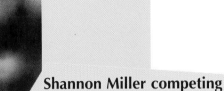

Shannon Miller competing in a floor exercise.

The Floor Exercises

Both men and women compete in the floor exercises on a carpet covered sprung area 12 metres square. The exercises include various dynamic tumbling skills (somersaults) linked together with spins or turns and balance movements. A free choice of instrumental music accompanies the women's performances, but the men perform without music.

The Vaulting Horse

The vaulting horse is also used by both the men and women. The men vault with the horse lengthways at a height of 135 cm and the women vault the horse sideways at a height of 120 cm. The modern vaulting horse has a sprung and padded upper surface to help the gymnasts bounce off. A springboard is used to help the gymnasts gain the speed and height needed to produce the modern exciting vaults.

You Ok Youl of Korea, on the vaulting horse.

7

The Gymnastics Apparatus

Women

In addition to the floor and vault exercises, women gymnasts also compete on two other apparatus.

The Beam

The balance beam is 500 cm long, 13 cm wide and 120 cm from the floor. The surface of the beam is slightly cushioned to make it easier on the feet. The exercise lasts between 70 and 90 seconds. The gymnast includes tumbling elements, leaps, spins or turns and balance movements.

The Asymmetric Bars

The uneven bars or **asymmetric bars** are two parallel bars set at different heights. Women gymnasts perform giant swings and **release and catch movements** and must also move from the high bar to the low bar.

Daniella Silivas in action on the balance beam.

Alexi Nemov showing his skill on the parallel bars.

Men

Men also perform on the floor and vault. They also do exercises on these four apparatus.

The Pommel Horse, or Sidehorse

The gymnast must support him- or herself on his or her hands while performing a series of complex circling movements. The circling movements may be performed with the legs together or in a straddled position known as a **Thomas flair**. The gymnast must also perform scissor-type exercises with the legs.

The Rings

The rings are suspended on wires from a frame and the gymnast demonstrates a variety of powerful swings combined with amazing strength exercises.

Parallel Bars

The parallel bars are 175 cm from the floor. The bars are quite flexible. The gymnast may swing above, below and across the bars and can let go while in the air during the exercise.

Horizontal Bars

The horizontal bar is a flexible metal bar and it is perhaps the most exciting of the men's apparatus. The exercise includes giant swings, moves close to the bar, and very spectacular release and re-grasp movements.

The Olympic Year

As the Olympic Games draw nearer, gymnasts' thoughts turn to what is almost certainly the most important year in their career. The senior gymnasts who may have helped the team to qualify hope to retain their place in the team. The younger gymnasts aim to edge their way into the team and achieve their dream of competing in the Olympic Games.

Making the Team

In the early part of the year selectors and coaches choose a squad of gymnasts who will train for the Olympic Games. From ten to twelve men and women gymnasts breathe a sigh of relief if they make it into the Olympic squad.

The gymnasts enter a year-long period of hard training and competitions. They hope to impress the selectors and eagerly await the final announcement of their national team.

A maximum of eight men and eight women gymnasts get the opportunity to compete as national team members.

Olympic Training

The national team coaches will draw up a programme of team training sessions and competitions. Each gymnast's personal coach will plan a training programme to prepare the gymnast for the Olympic Games. No detail will be forgotten.

The coach has a vital role in the training schedule of a gymnast.

Training programme

The programme will include:

- **choreography**
- **flexibility** training
- strength training
- perfection of skills
- mental preparation
- rest and recovery periods
- **nutrition** (food and drink)
- health and fitness checks.

Training Diary

Each gymnast usually keeps a personal training diary and writes down all the details of their training sessions. This helps the coach to measure how well the gymnast is training and feeling. Encouraging phrases such as 'Be strong' and 'Don't give in' may be included to help support the gymnast.

Team Kit

One of any gymnast's proudest moments is receiving the team kit. Representing your country alongside other famous athletes brings its own special excitement. Each gymnast will also have their own favourite training kit. Some competitors can be very superstitious and always train wearing certain 'lucky' garments!

The Gymnast's Diet

Gymnasts must have time to rest and time to eat the foods which provide the 'fuel' to help them train hard. Gymnasts must be strong but also control their body weight. They need to take great care to eat the right amount of food in a proper balanced diet.

Gymnasts must eat a variety of foods for different purposes. They need energy foods such as rice, pasta and potatoes. To build their bodies they need white meat, fish, dairy products and a little red meat. To complete a balanced diet, they also need fruit and vegetables, low fat, high fibre foods and plenty of liquids, particularly water.

Gymnasts need to eat one and a half hours before training to digest the food properly. They shouldn't drink carbonated drinks before a training session or a competition. After training, gymnasts need to eat again to rebuild energy.

The men in the British team celebrate a winning performance.

Peak of Fitness

Gymnasts must be at their peak of fitness if they are to compete well and enjoy the experience of a lifetime. The final stages of training will be carefully planned by their coaches to ensure that the gymnasts feel ready for the big event.

Did you know?

- **The Olympic village will host around 12 000 athletes and officials.**

- **Many athletes will arrive at the Games at least one week before their event to acclimatize and prepare for their competition.**

- **About 200 gymnasts will compete in the gymnastics event.**

- **The gymnasts will train twice each day while at the Olympic Games.**

- **They will practise in training halls and will have only two chances to train in the competition hall.**

- **Gymnastics is one of the most popular Olympic sports and there will be a great demand for tickets. Every 'session' will be sold out far in advance of the Games.**

- **The Olympic village has its own restaurants and cinema.**

Final Stages of Training

The last few weeks of training will consist of:

- practising the competition exercises
- **peaking** or increasing the training load to a maximum, two weeks before the event
- **tapering** or reducing the training load to allow the gymnast to prepare mentally for the event
- special strength training
- practice competitions
- learning to deal with fears and emotions
- thinking about the **goals** or aims – being positive
- working through 'what if' situations to prepare for any problems.

Gymnasts make the most of opportunities to train.

Gymnasts take time to relax, too. Here some American, British and Chinese gymnasts visit the koala bears!

Saying Goodbye

The last home gym session is over and it is time to pack the travel bags. The excitement grows as the national team members pack their:

- team kit
- team uniform
- competition clothing
- hand grips
- training kit
- lucky mascot
- books and tapes
- leisure clothes.

Then it's goodbye to friends and family and off to the Olympic Games!

Journey to a Dream

The dream begins to turn to reality for gymnastics team members as they meet fellow athletes at the airport, surrounded by cameras and people wishing them good luck. During the long flight the team doctors urge the squad to rest, relax, sleep, keep moving all their joints, drink liquids and eat the correct foods.

Olympic Village

Security in the Olympic village is always very strict and competitors are given their own passport that allows them to enter the village. Only the athletes, coaches and team officials are allowed in.

Gymnasts will soon be joining the others roaming the village, meeting athletes from all over the world, chatting and making new friends.

Training at the Olympic Games

Preparation

Team meetings are held to discuss the travel arrangements, meal times and training times for the squad. The order in which the gymnasts compete will be decided by the team coach.

The coach has a great responsibility in ensuring that team morale remains high and that the gymnasts do not become too nervous and lose their confidence.

Pre-competition Training

The pre-competition training schedule is very important. The coach will want to see good performances from the squad so that confidence remains high.

The coaches and gymnasts will be interested to see how well the other teams are training but this must not affect their own concentration and **focus**.

Ivan Ivankov shows the way on the pommel horse.

The First Competition

The first competition is perhaps the most difficult event. The gymnasts compete as individuals in different groups. Then their individual total scores are added together to produce the team total and team **ranking**. In the Atlanta Games, the gymnasts will perform compulsory exercises as the first event.

Competitors arrive at the arena by bus from the village. They are taken first to the training hall. Warming up and practising in the warm-up gym eases the nerves. The gymnasts try to stay calm, relaxed and confident.

However, when they finally enter the arena, the lights, the crowd noise and the colour – all cause the pulse to begin to race. But this is the time to stay calm – concentrate and think positive.

All the gymnasts will try hard to compete well for their team mates and the nervous tension will be high.

Team Support

After the event the gymnasts will reflect on how well they performed – there may be feelings of joy or there may be a little disappointment. However, the coaches will give their support and the gymnasts will encourage their team members as they compete. The coaches will calculate the team rankings even before the score system can announce the team scores!

Tatiana Lisenkko soars between the asymmetric bars.

Voluntary Exercises

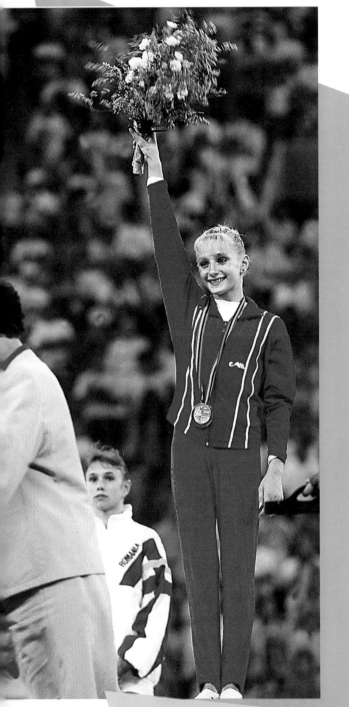

Tatiana Gutsu proudly receives her award in the 1992 Games.

A Team Effort

In the second event the gymnasts will all perform voluntary exercises on each apparatus. They work as a team, competing according to the team's ranking from the first day of the competition. The highest ranked teams compete in the last rounds of the competition.

The spectacular voluntary exercises attract a capacity crowd and the noise and excitement is immense. Great team spirit is shown as the gymnasts and coaches urge each other to do well.

After the event great feelings of relief, and maybe some disappointment, will be felt as the gymnasts and coaches wait to discover their team ranking – and who will become the Olympic Team Champions.

The Awards Ceremony

The day climaxes with the awards ceremony for the three medallists. The national anthem for the winning team is played and the flag is raised. Pictures of the winning team will be beamed around the world.

For some, this will be the end of Olympic competition but they will know they came to the Olympic Games and gave their best. There is no time for resting as the top gymnasts are quickly back in the training gym to prepare for the next event, the all-around competition for the top 36 gymnasts.

The All-around Title

The combined totals from the first and second competitions determine the qualifiers for the all-around event. The top 36 men and the top 36 women qualify.

A maximum of three gymnasts from each qualifying country may compete in the all-around event. There is no carry over score from previous qualifying competitions so the gymnasts start with a zero score.

Each gymnast performs their voluntary exercises on all the apparatus – six pieces for the men and four pieces for the women.

The gymnast with the highest total score becomes the Olympic All-around Champion.

In the all-around event the the gymnasts often try more difficult exercises to gain more points. There is tremendous excitement and audiences enjoy these closely contested events.

Close Competitions

Just one major mistake can rule out a contender for the title. To be the Olympic champion is every gymnast's dream and very few will have more than one attempt at winning the title.

Often the title will be won by a very small margin.

Vitaly Scherbo also celebrated a prize-winning performance in Barcelona in 1992.

The Last Day of Competition

This day is almost like a festival of gymnastics where the world's best gymnasts on each apparatus compete for the individual titles. This is the only day where the men and women compete in the arena at the same time.

Individual Apparatus Finals

The highest ranked gymnasts on each apparatus from the first two competitions qualify for this event.

The top eight male qualifiers in the floor exercise, pommel horse (side horse), rings, vaults, parallel bars and horizontal bar compete to become Olympic champion.

The top eight women qualifiers in vault, assymetric bars (uneven bars), beam and floor exercise will compete for the individual apparatus medals in those events. A maximum of two gymnasts from any country can qualify for the finals.

He Xuemei at her peak on the asymmetric bars.

Alexi Nemov,
the champion-class
Russian gymnast.

Most Spectacular

The individual apparatus
finals are often the most
spectacular, since the
gymnasts involved
frequently attempt their
most difficult routines.
It is possible that the
Olympic all-around
champion may not win
all of the apparatus titles
because a gymnast with
exceptional skills in one
particular event may win
that title. Only great
gymnasts qualify for all
of the individual
apparatus finals.

The audience at the
individual apparatus
finals creates a festival
atmosphere which
provides great motivation
for the gymnasts. There is
often a more light-hearted
atmosphere and this may
help the gymnasts to
relax and produce
exceptional exercises.

Olympic Dreams

The greatest honour in any sport is to win an Olympic gold medal. Every gymnast will have dreamed of becoming the Olympic Champion or at least of taking part in the Olympics. Millions of people have the dream but only a fortunate few will have that great honour of becoming an **Olympian**.

The long, hard road to becoming a top gymnast requires dedication and determination.

Getting Started

Most gymnasts start training when they are six to ten years old. Women gymnasts are usually from fifteen to eighteen years old when they first compete in the Olympic Games. The men require greater physical strength and they are usually eighteen to twenty-four years old when they are at their best.

Mary Lou Retton, a USA Olympian gymnast.

Useful hints

- Join a gymnastics club with qualified and experienced coaches.

- Talk to your parents/guardian and your coach about what you wish to achieve.

- Follow the guidance of your coach very carefully and positively.

- Work hard on flexibility, strength and basic gymnastics movements.

- With the help of your coach set yourself challenging goals.

- Above all have fun and enjoy your sport.

Training Time

The top gymnasts such as Britain's world silver medallist Neil Thomas started training with only two to three sessions a week.

As their strength grows, gymnasts gradually increase the training time up to 30 hours a week at the height of their career.

Gymnasts will train two or maybe three times a day but coaches vary the training load to ensure that there is no over training.

The Young Gymnast's Healthy Lifestyle

The young gymnast will spend many hours in the gymnasium and their lifestyle will be planned around the gym and school time.

Gymnastic training helps concentration which improves the ability to study at school. It also helps develop self-confidence. The many training hours means that friends of gymnasts are mostly other gymnasts, but they may be from all around the world.

Gymnasts relax just like any young person, by playing other sports, watching films or listening to music.

Neil Thomas, a British gymnast, at the 1992 Games.

A healthy, balanced diet is very important to a young gymnast and so is plenty of sleep to help the body to recover from the hard training.

The parents of young gymnasts must have the **dedication** to encourage their child to lead a healthy lifestyle.

The Coach's Task

The gymnastics coach must carefully plan a training programme which will help the young child to become an international gymnast. The great Romanian gymnast Nadia Comaneci was guided through the years of physical growth from young child to young woman by her coaches Pozgar and Karoli.

Training Plans

The coach plans a training programme to ensure success for the gymnast. The plan will include the gradual development of:

- flexibility in all parts of the body to allow skills to be learned
- strength – for speed and endurance
- basic gymnastics movements, correctly performed since the advanced skills are built upon the quality of the basic movements
- choreography – to develop style, strength, control and more interesting movements
- landing drills – to ensure that the gymnast can land safely

Nadia Comaneci, fluid and graceful in motion.

- **rebound skills** – using the trampoline to develop awareness in the air
- learning and perfection of single movements, combined movements and full competition exercises
- mental preparation to learn how to deal with the stress of competition.

The gymnastics arena in Los Angeles, 1984.

Competitions

The real test of a gymnast is performing exercises in a match or competition. It requires many hours of training to perfect the exercises but the gymnast also needs great confidence to perform in front of an audience and judges.

This competition experience will be developed over a long period of time and by involvement in many competition events. The coach will enter the gymnast into progressively more demanding situations to prepare them for big events.

Four Stages of Development

1 Exercises are practised many times in training sessions, and the coach counts the number of successful attempts.

2 Coach and team-mates watch the performance of the exercise.

3 The gymnast takes part in a practice or control competition with a judge scoring the exercise.

4 Less important events are used to measure the level of 'readiness' of the gymnast before the big event.

Progressive Events

As the gymnasts gain experience they will learn more difficult exercises and will progress to higher level competitions or matches.

Events will range from beginner level through to intermediate level and advanced level.

There are age-controlled events at school, club, county, regional, national and international level.

Team Selection

The coaches and team selectors will study the progress of every gymnast and will invite the best gymnasts at national events to join the national squads. From these squads the Olympic team will be chosen.

History of the Olympics

The first modern Olympic Games were held in Athens, Greece in 1896. Men's gymnastics was one of nine sports included in these games and the first Olympic Champion was Alfred Flatow from Germany.

The women's individual all-around championship was not included until the 1952 Helsinki Olympic Games. Maria Gorokhouskia (USSR) became the first women's Olympic Champion.

The Japanese Men

The Rome Olympics held in 1960 saw the Japanese men's team take the first of five consecutive Olympic team titles.

The USSR Success Story

In the women's event the might of the USSR dominated the team competition. The Soviet women's team won the Olympic title from 1952 through to 1984. During this period there were many great champions.

Mexican Hat Dance

In the 1968 Mexico Olympics the very powerful and consistent Vera Caslavska from Czechoslovakia, stole the show with a floor routine performed to the time of the 'Mexican Hat Dance'.

The Korbut Games

The 1972 Munich Olympic Games were called the `Korbut Games' because of the way the television media took to the young Olga Korbut. Olga won the floor and beam titles but surprisingly the all-around title was won by her Soviet team-mate Ludmila Tourischeva.

The Perfect Ten

At the 1976 Montreal Games a string of 'perfect ten' scores were awarded to Nadia Comaneci of Romania. This remarkable young woman burst onto the scene and started a new era in women's gymnastics.

Olga Korbut captivated the world at the Games in 1972.

24

Moscow 1980

The Moscow Olympic Games were remembered for two reasons. First the USSR won the men's and women's team titles and both the all-around titles. Second, these were also the Games that introduced the new and spectacular 'release and catch' movements by the men on the horizontal bars.

The American Dream

Sadly, the 1984 Los Angeles Games were boycotted by many of the top East European teams.

The exciting Chinese gymnasts Li Ning, Lou Yun and Tong Fei joined the Olympic events for the first time. The men's title was won by the very popular Koji Gushiken (Japan).

The USA men won the team title by 0.6 points from China while the dynamic American Mary Lou Retton won the women's title by just 0.05 points from the great Romanian Ecaterina Szabo.

Seoul 1988

The mighty Soviet gymnasts returned to win both the men's and women's team events and both all-around titles.

Vladimir Atemov (USSR) won the men's title and three individual titles to make it a total of five gold medals.

Barcelona Fiesta 1992

The audience at these 'friendly' games witnessed the former Soviet gymnasts competing as individuals from their home countries.

However the ex-Soviet gymnasts competed as a team under the title of the Commonwealth of Independent States (CIS) and won both the men's and women's team titles.

The gymnast who made the biggest impact in Barcelona was the great Vitaly Scherbo (Biela Russia) who won the men's all-around event to add to the team gold and four individual apparatus titles. Tatiana Gutsu (Ukraine) fought a huge battle with Shannon Miller (USA) to win by just 0.012 marks.

Atlanta 1996

The gymnasts to look out for are Grigori Misutin, Ivan Ivankov, Dominique Dawes, Shannon Miller and Svetlana Khorkina. But there are sure to be some surprises and new faces.

Ruslam Charipov, the Ukrainian gymnast, swings around the bars.

Gymnastics Innovators

Many of the gymnastics movements used today are named after the gymnast who first peformed the movement in a major event.

Stalder Circle

As far back as 1948, the Swiss gymnast Josef Stalder introduced the clear straddle circle to become the Olympic champion on the horizontal bar. The technique has been refined, but the movement is still performed today.

Endo Circle

The great Japanese gymnast Yukio Endo peformed the Stalder circle in a forwards direction. The movement was named after him and it is still a popular element in both men's and women's bar exercises.

Diomidov Turn

In the 1960s the Soviet gymnast Sergei Diomidov surprised the world by performing a swinging full turn in a one arm handstand position on the parallel bars. This movement still retains a medium level difficulty in modern day gymnastics.

Release and Catch

The 1970s saw the greatest change in men's gymnastics when the spectacular and dangerous-looking release and catch elements were first seen. Here are a few.

Movement	Created by
Geinger-Salto	Eberhart Geinger (Germany)
Deltchev	Stoyan Deltchev (Bulgaria)
Tkachev	Alexander Tkachev (USSR)
Gaylord 1 and 2	Mitch Gaylord (USA)

Grigori Misutin in action.

Women First

The majority of new movements have been developed by the men gymnasts but there are two notable exceptions.

Karen Jaeger (Germany) developed the Jaeger-Salto – a straddled front somersault and catch on the women's bars. Natalia Yurchenko (USSR) amazed the world with a round-off back hardspring vault.

The Jaeger-Salto and the Yurchenko vault have also been adopted by men gymnasts.

The Two Thomases

Kurt Thomas (USA) and Neil Thomas (GB) have both introduced remarkable movements.

Kurt Thomas developed the straddled circle on pommel horse (side horse) – the 'Thomas Flairs'.

The amazing Straight Front Salto with two twists on floor performed by Neil is known simply as the 'Thomas'.

Beam Acrobatics

Despite the beam being only 13 cm wide women gymnasts are able to perform amazing **acrobatic** movements on the beam.

Often three tumbling skills are linked directly together. Spectacular movements are also performed across and around the beam as well as along its length.

Li-Li of China makes an arc in the air.

 Facts and Figures

Vladimir Artemov, one of the few men to have won four gold medals in one Olympic Games.

Record Holders

The most amazing gymnastic record is held by the USSR women's team. They have not been beaten as a team in the Olympic Games since they first took the title in 1952. They had eight wins in a row, then they did not attend in 1984 but regained the title in 1992 competing as the Commonwealth Independent States.

The Japanese men's team won the team title five times in a row from 1960 to 1976.

Vitaly Scherbo has won the highest number of gold medals in one Olympic Games. He won six gold medals at the Barcelona Games.

Gold Medals

Four men have won four gymnastics gold medals in one Olympic Games. They are:

- Boris Shakhlin (USSR – 1960)
- Akinori Nakayama (Japan – 1968)
- Nikolai Andrianov (USSR – 1976)
- Vladimir Artemov (USSR – 1988).

To retain the all-round Olympic title is an amazing feat and this has been achieved by:

- Alberto Braglia (Italy – 1908/12)
- Viktor Chukarin (USSR – 1952/56)
- Larisa Latynina (USSR – 1956/60)
- Vera Caslavska (Tch – 1964/68)
- Sawao Kato (Japan – 1968/72).

The great Czechoslovakian woman gymnast, Vera Caslavska, won three gold medals in two different Olympic Games (1964 and 1968).

Apparatus Changes

The gymnastics apparatus has been changed and developed to allow new movements to be learned and to reduce the risk of injury to the gymnast.

The more important changes include:

- the sprung and carpeted floor area

- the modern sprung vaulting horse and springboard

- the shock-absorbing landing mats

- fibreglass uneven bars and the change from oval to round bars

- **handguards**/grips with a small plastic dowel to give improved grip on the bars or rings

- foam-filled landing areas in training gyms.

Sandy Woolsey moving between the parallel bars.

New Techniques

The changes to the apparatus and the improved preparation of the gymnasts has helped them to perform amazing movements including triple somersaults, **double somersaults** with **multiple twists**, spectacular release and catch movements and amazing strength movements.

No doubt the future of gymnastics will be as exciting and full of developments as its past has been.

Glossary

acclimatize adjust to heat, humidity and high altitude

acrobatics a combination of somersaults and overswings

all-around event the combined compulsory and optional event scores

asymmetric bars uneven parallel bars set at different heights

choreography the dance and body movement elements used in a floor exercise

Compulsory exercises set sequence of movements in the first event that the gymnast must complete

consistent being able to repeat an exercise accurately over and over again

dedication being fully committed to something

Deltchev back somersault with a half turn in a straddled position to the recatch the bar

double somersault two complete rotations performed in the air in one movement

dynamic very powerful movement or action

Endo circle a straddled circle moving to a handstand on the bar

flexibility the range of movement in a joint of the body

focus to concentrate upon something very hard

Gaylord a double forward somersault over the bar then recatching the bar

Geinger-Salto a backward somersault with a half turn to regrasp the bar

giant swing a complete rotation around a bar with the body extended in a handstand position

goals aims, ambitions or targets

handguard (handgrip) a leather strap worn on the hands to provide a grip on the apparatus and to reduce wear on the hands

judges officials who assess and score the performance of the gymnasts

mental preparation preparation to deal with the nervous effects of competition and to think about how movements are performed

morale confidence and spirit of a gymnast

multiple twist more than one turn around the vertical axis of the gymnast's body

nutrition the advantages we gain from the food we eat

Olympian an athlete or gymnast who has competed in the Olympic Games

optional exercises a sequence of voluntary exercises performed by each gymnast

peaking increasing the training load to a maximum at a particular time

podium the platform on which the gymnastics equipment is erected

psyching deliberately building positive mental preparation

ranking the order in which a team is placed according to their scores

rebound skills movements which are learned on a trampoline

release and catch movement a movement in which the gymnast releases the grasp on the bar, somersaults and then catches the bar again

Stalder circle a backward straddled circle leading to a handstand on the bar

tapering gradually reducing or tapering the training load just before a competition

Thomas flair circles around the hands in a handstand in a split legs position

Tkachev a backward straddled release and catch movement performed over the bar

twist a turn around the vertical axis of the body

Index

Numbers in plain type (23) refer to the text; numbers in italic (23) refer to a caption.